BEHOLD THE TURTLE

Barbara Jolovitz
&
Kenneth A. Walsh

Michael Boardman, Illustrator

Behold the Turtle

ISBN 978-0-945980-78-0

Library of Congress Control Number: 2014936816

North Country Press
Unity, Maine

"Behold the turtle. He makes progress only when he sticks his neck out."

James Bryant Conant, 1893-1978
President, Harvard University 1933-1953

DEDICATION

We wish to dedicate this book to the memory of founders Lester Jolovitz, Richard Hawkes and George Keller whose visions and hope for children to have a fun and safe summer experience have been realized in their founding of Camp Tracy on McGrath Pond in Oakland, Maine.

The generosity of the New Balance Foundation, the Heritage Circle, the Board of Directors of the Boys & Girls Clubs and the YMCA of Greater Waterville, and countless others have enabled those visions and hopes to become realities. We honor all of you.

The future of Camp Tracy is bright and exciting and will continue to provide the fun and safe place for children as envisioned by Lester, Dick and George.

Ken Walsh and Barbara Jolovitz

ACKNOWLEDGEMENTS

We wish to acknowledge the following people and businesses whose gifts to Camp Tracy have played a major role in making it the unique place where children are safe and happy in their summer camp experience. We also wish to acknowledge the Camp Tracy staff whose dedication has been key for the camp to run smoothly and successfully. Thank you.

Four Seasons Lodge
    New Balance Foundation
        Sponsored in part by: the Gaunce family, Mike Runser,
        Waterville physicians, and Cianbro Corp.

55-foot Climbing Tower
    Dead River Company

Beach House
    Peter Alfond

High/Low Ropes Course
    L.L.Bean

Family Lean-To's
    Walsh/Hart Family (Thomas & Avis Hart/Arthur & Theresa Walsh)
    Karter Family (Chuck and Alli Karter)
    Jabar Family (Joe & Bridget Jabar, Jr.)
    Basavappa Family (Prakash & Nandini)
    Hammond Lumber

Tennis Court
    Dorie Hawkes

Walking Trails
    Barbezat

Archery Range
    Beck Family

Jolovitz Outdoor Theater
    Lester and Barbara Jolovitz

Fenway Park
    Harold Alfond

Kinder Camp Building
    George Keller

Harold Alfond Turf Field
    John Huard

Cabins
    Unity Foundation
        Honoring:
        • Bert G. & Coral B. Clifford
        • Hon. Donald H. Marden
        • Ralph A. Martin
        • Donald Foster
        • Gregory Powell
        • Good Will-Hinckley

Pavillion
    Plum Creek

Bickford Bathhouse
    Dan and Jane Bickford

Well House
    A.E. Hodsdon

Flag Pole
    Kenneth and Shirley Eskelund

Ronald McDonald & Eskelund Cabin
    Ronald McDonald House Charities of Maine
    and Kenneth Eskelund Trust Fund

Fire Circle
    Steve and Alice King

Table of Contents

CHELYDRA SERPENTINA SERPENTINA: TURTLE

This is a tale of the discovery of my distant family of giant tortoises, Geochelone elephantopus, discovered by Spaniards in the 16th Century on some islands in the Pacific Ocean. Those discoverers named the islands Galapagos after my cousins as galapago is an old Spanish word for tortoise. My cousins have the longest life span of any animal on earth, some living up to 150 years.

The second visit of note was in 1835 by the Englishman Charles Darwin and that is the one that made my cousins and the Galapagos Islands famous though we had already been on Earth for over 400 million years. We remember staying out of the way of dinosaurs as they roamed about.

Unlike my Galapagos cousins who were discovered by man, I made the discovery of man in the mid-1960's as they were about to enter the 64 acres of land and the lake I inhabited in Oakland, Maine. You see, I am a snapping turtle with the exotic name of Chelydra serpentina serpentina. The name serpentina indicates I have a highly mobile snake-like neck which in no way warns that I also snap and hiss. I do like to live on land but I often live in fresh water, the ocean or brackish ponds and I like to eat plants, insects and fish. My lifestyle and diet differ somewhat from those of my tortoise cousins who live almost entirely out of water and eat only grasses, flowers, weeds and cactus.

As I said, I discovered man. One day as I was enjoying my paradise a car stopped nearby and three men got out and retrieved three hatchets from out of the trunk. Keeping my distance, I wondered what three men dressed in suits and ties carrying hatchets were going to do in my sanctuary. "Let's go, Lester and Dick." "We'll follow you, George." Now I knew their names. I continued to watch at a distance as many of my family became known for being a culinary delight: turtle soup. With hatchets and my slow gait, distance as well as discretion was important.

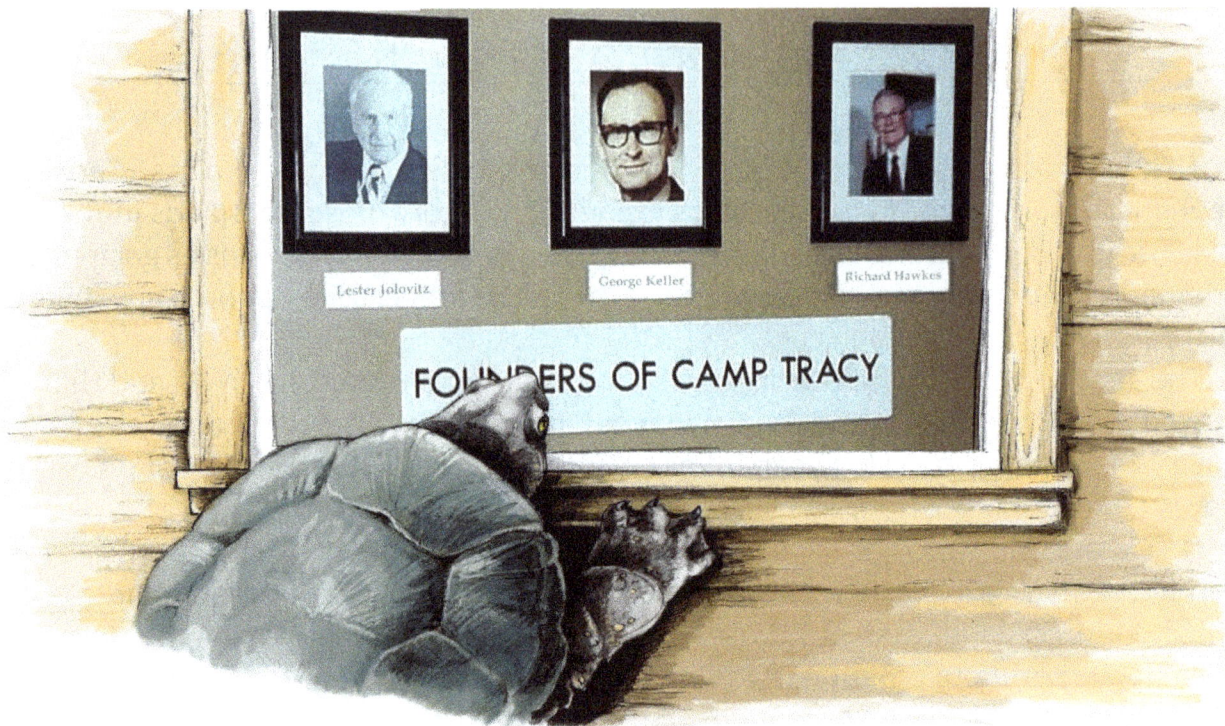

The men talked as they hacked their way to my lake. They were there to see if my land might be suitable as a YMCA summer retreat for children. The man called George was head of the YMCA. Mrs. Tracy who shared the land with me and actually owned the land wanted to sell it. She did not know I even existed. The men thought the land most suitable and it was decided that the YMCA would buy the land from Mrs. Tracy. The land became known as Camp Tracy on March 22, 1968 when Mrs. Tracy deeded it to the YMCA.

For several years, I watched children come and go on a path to and from the lake. Then one spring, there was so much activity that I stayed in my lake for my safety and where I could observe what was happening.

A two-level Four Seasons Lodge was built where meetings could take place on the top level, and on the lower level there was a kitchen and rooms set up for sleeping. The top level had a convenient patio all around it so I walked up and looked into the meeting room where I saw photographs of Lester (Jolovitz), George (Keller) and Richard (Hawkes) with a sign under their photographs saying they were the founders of Camp Tracy.

Then a baseball field started to emerge. Again from a safe distance I heard comments that it was two-thirds the size of a place called Fenway Park in Boston where the Red Sox play baseball and that this field would have a green monster wall just like Fenway Park. A MONSTER IN MY SANCTUARY! Perhaps the children who play baseball will keep the monster at bay by feeding it home runs.

Over the years I have been spotted by campers when I poked my nose out of the water or as I patrolled my habitat. Sometimes when I have been spotted patrolling, people have picked me up by my shell to take my picture and suspend me ungracefully with my underside to the camera. Most distressful. I wouldn't mind a picture of me on the ground as it would show my elegant shell and not my less attractive under self.

I hear campers referring to me as "Myrtle the turtle." Children like to rhyme names with objects although I don't remember Maine's famous poet Henry Wadsworth Longfellow's children's poems doing that. If I were to have a name, I would prefer it be my lovely Latin name but simply Turtle without any rhyming is fine. My tortoise family also likes to be called simply Tortoise.

George and I had a special relationship. He loved to swim and he and Mrs. George would come to our lake to swim every day during the summer in the late afternoon. I did not hide from George and his wife as I knew they loved my habitat as much as I did and I felt safe with them nearby. George would acknowledge me with a knowing smile. Very often they would be humming as they strolled to the lake and Beethoven's 7th Symphony became my favorite. I eventually caught up with them at the lake and watched them enjoying their swim. When George finished his swim, he would look all around the lake just as I do and then the three of us would walk up the trail to his car and they were gone.

George and I shared a concern that Camp Tracy might develop too fast and there would be buildings set up which would not fit in with the rustic feeling of our habitat. As it turned out, as the trees were taken down, they were taken to a mill to be made into shingles which were used on every building except for the original two. George need not have worried.

A few years ago, I watched three cabins being built which could sleep 50 campers. They were all sided with shingles made from the trees cleared to make room for the cabins. George would have liked their rustic look and the fact that the trees had a new life.

The first year the cabins were completed, several children all the way from China stayed in them! I enjoyed watching the children who were at the lake for the first time. They had never seen a lake before as all of them had grown up in a large city. They shivered as they put their feet in the clear cool water but laughed at being able to see their feet in the water. It didn't take them long to get used to the lake and enjoy it as much as the local campers. The Chinese children adapted quickly to my beautiful world as they understood the balance of the woods to the lake to the sky from the Tao teachings of their ancient ancestors.

One day, Dick was not feeling well so he did not come to Camp Tracy with Lester and George but there was a third man with them called Ken. Ken seemed important and George confirmed it. He and George talked about youth activities in the community and a merger of the Boys & Girls Clubs where Ken worked and the Greater Waterville Area YMCA where George worked. Ken and George discussed ideas of the merger and how two organizations together could make a strong impact on youth and families. They were thankful to have the financial assistance of Harold Alfond who became the catalyst in bringing the two entities together. It was the only merger of its kind in the country and it became known as the Alfond Youth Center, with Ken as its CEO. The merger reminded me of how two rivals, Mike Torrez and Bucky Dent, worked together for the benefit of children they could help with their baseball expertise.

A group of individual supporters of Camp Tracy became known as the Heritage Circle, with Lester as its first president. Ken realized how much Lester loved Camp Tracy. As the Heritage Circle president, Lester suggested Heritage Circle members visit my habitat. Lester would conduct board meetings at Camp Tracy. He wasted no time in getting things together and when our dear friend George died, he took over for him, too. Ken told me that before George died, he told George about a scholarship Lester had established in his name. George was special and loved by all of us.

I knew about Dick Hawkes from his foray into my habitat with Lester and George, but I did not know about Mrs. Hawkes.

Dorie, as she was called, coached athletics at Waterville High School and was very involved in athletics at the YMCA where she introduced a children's gymnastic program and helped support women's programs there during the late 1960's.

As chairwoman of Camp Tracy, the guidelines she instituted for the camp's operation were based on her philosophy that every child has a need for learning.

In recognition of their parents' dedication to the YMCA, Dick and Dorie Hawkes' daughters gifted Camp Tracy the Dorie Hawkes Tennis Court, which reflected their mother's participation in and interest in sports.

In the past five years, there have been tennis tournaments played by members of the Heritage Circle, but future tournaments will be played by Camp Tracy children.

Though Dick and Dorie never played tennis at the Dorie Hawkes Tennis Court, they were never outmatched in their dedication to the YMCA and Camp Tracy.

One day as I was watching a tennis match from where I thought I was safe, something whizzed close to my head and I immediately ducked into my shell. It was an errant arrow from the archery target next to the tennis courts.

Archeologists have determined that bows and arrows have been used for hunting since 50,000 B.C.E. and recent ancient history finds the Egyptians using them against the Persians in 5000 B.C.E. The Egyptian arrows were made from reeds bound with linen thread and tipped with flint heads which took care of the Persians handily.

As centuries went by, it was decided that archery was more a sport than a lethal weapon and in 1900, archery was in the Olympic Games for the first time and in the 1904 and 1908 games, women were allowed to compete.

The arrow that sailed over my head was a new type of arrow, lighter and stronger, which increased its speed and accuracy and made an errant arrow a very scary missile to a turtle. After my fright, I seized the day by roaming my Camp Tracy habitat, nibbling berries and relaxing with a quiet swim in my cool, clear, lovely lake. Then, as I do at the end of every day, I reflected on the day and my good fortune to have had my shell — my carapace — to duck into which saved my life. With that in mind, I will from this day forward refer to seizing the day as carapace diem so I never forget.

When the campers are not at camp, I sometimes use their Down Trail to get to the water and their Up Trail to get away from the water. Those are the trails George, Mrs. George and I used to walk together when they came to Camp Tracy for their swims.

The Nature Trail around Camp Tracy is a part of my habitat I especially enjoy. I visit with Cladonia cristatella, the red-topped British Soldier lichen named for the red caps British soldiers wore in the Revolutionary War and Cladonia rangiferina, reindeer moss lichen so named because it looks like reindeer antlers. It was a survival food for Native Americans and today is the favorite food of reindeer and caribou and is an occasional nibble for me. I will often have a healthy summer supper of sweet juicy blackberries and a mosquito I find along the Nature Trail.

In 1758, Carlus Linnaeus, a Swedish botanist, physician and zoologist, ascribed Latin names to plants, or flora, after Flora the Roman goddess of flowers, and fauna to animals, after Fauna, the Roman goddess of wild nature. He also Latinized his own name from Carl von Linné. By choosing Latin as a universal method of naming all living things, a common point of reference was established. And, of course, I am grateful to him for my Latin name: Chelydra serpentina serpentina

THE CHALLENGING THREE

There are three activities which challenge the campers as well as me. I would like to conquer them but my shell limits my athletic agility. Also, I am a coward and I do not have a wizard in my habitat to help me overcome my cowardice. However, there is one challenge I might accept and that is climbing the 55' Climbing Wall which looks to me as tall as Mt. Katahdin, Maine's tallest mountain. The campers scurry up and down it with much ease.

I will do it. On the next moonlit starry night, I will put leg after leg into the slots where the campers put their feet and then push with their legs to straighten up and get their hands into the next set of slots. I will do the same and get to the top of the Climbing Wall. And from the top, I will look out at my entire lake bathed in moonlight, twinkling stars and silhouettes of Maine's stately pine trees. I will not need a wizard after all.

I will not cajole myself into doing the Cat Walk or the Squirrel Swing. I have seen the frightened campers when it is their turn. I have also seen the same campers so excited and proud of themselves for doing it that they run to the end of a waiting line of campers for their turn to do it again.

The Cat Walk consists of climbing up one of two 30-ft. pine trees to which a log and ropes are anchored to the top. Climbers must walk to the middle of the log, fall a quarter of the way down unassisted, though wearing a harness for safety. Once they are suspended between the logs, they are lowered to the bottom by the harness.

My squirrel neighbors never go near the Squirrel Swing. Campers start by sitting on a chair that is on the ground between two 50-ft. posts and then they get hoisted about two-thirds of the way up. From there, they swing to the top of one post, back to the middle and then swing to the top of the other post. After doing that a few times, they are eased down.

Brave campers, I applaud you for your courage.

One summer a Native American Wilderness survival week was held at Camp Tracy. Chief Barry Dana of the Penobscot Nation was there and he taught the campers how to build huts, what berries were safe to eat and how to track animals. By this time, I had become adept in my own survival skills and Chief Dana did not find my tracks. However, Chief Dana knew about me and that Camp Tracy was my habitat. He told the campers that the turtle was the spirit of the south wind.

The Penobscot Native Americans live on Indian Island across the river from Old Town, Maine, but Native Americans have been living in the Penobscot River Basin in Maine for 11,000 years, surviving on animals, fish, shellfish, berries, birds, nuts, and vegetables they have grown. The famous beautiful sweet grass baskets woven by the Native American women on Indian Island are woven from grasses they gather, dry and color with native dyes. Equally as famous as the sweet grass baskets are the birch bark canoes built on Indian Island.

It was very exciting having Chief Dana in my habitat for the week. He taught the campers to respect the woods and its gifts for survival the same way every Native American respects its woods and its gifts which have enabled them to survive for so many thousands of years.

Football has come to Camp Tracy. Children between the ages of 8 and 12 come for a week of training camp to learn techniques from the legendary player and coach John Huard as well as from professional players. I watched with fascination as the children jumped through roped-off squares, threw and caught footballs and did a lot of running around on the artificial turf play field which was a gift to Camp Tracy from Coach Huard.

John Huard grew up in Waterville and was a member of the Boys & Girls Clubs along with Harold Alfond's son Teddy. Mr. Alfond recognized that John was an excellent athlete and knowing John could use financial help, he provided a scholarship for John to go to Kent's Hill, a prep school in Maine. At the University of Maine, John was a star linebacker and was scouted and drafted by the Denver Broncos. His playing career was followed by coaching in Montreal and Toronto. When he retired, he coached at Kent's Hill and now donates his time to coaching at Camp Tracy.

As is the wont of recipients of kindnesses such as Harold Alfond's in providing a scholarship for John, those recipients want to do something in return to show their appreciation to their benefactor. John did just that in his gift of the artificial turf play field to Camp Tracy as thanks to Harold Alfond for his gracious gift. Coach Huard had not forgotten.

JOLOVITZ OUTDOOR THEATER

My world has a stage, an amphitheater with the name Jolovitz Outdoor Theater on a rustic board above the stage. A simple stage has been replaced with a new stage, dressing rooms, spotlights, microphones, a wooden barrel roof over the stage and outside lighting. It looks like a miniature of the Boston Pops Esplanade shell.

Campers gather at the theater at the end of each day and on every other Thursday, the day before the end of their two-week camp adventure, they perform skits for their parents and families which they have written with their counselors. The additional benches put in when the theater was going up are filled up with families enjoying the performances. At the end of the performances, everyone gathers around the Steve King Fire Circle beside the theater. The first time I saw the smoke rising from the fire circle I wondered if signals were being sent to Chief Dana.

Steve King grew up in Waterville and spent many years at the Boys & Girls Clubs. His working years were at New Balance where he was in the Human Resources Department. He was pleased when the Boys & Girls Clubs and the YMCA merged to become the Alfond Youth Center and was proud to become a board member of the Center. He could see the potential of Camp Tracy and talked about it at New Balance. New Balance became so excited about Camp Tracy that the New Balance Foundation issued a $1 million challenge to the Alfond Youth Center. The Four Seasons Lodge was the first building built with funds from that challenge and several buildings followed. Steve and Ken used to walk together around Camp Tracy, talking about and looking at the results of the generosity of so many people who responded to the New Balance challenge. Their gifts gave my habitat many more opportunities for campers to have a great camp experience.

The Rangers are the 11- and 12-year-old campers who come to Camp Tracy and are old enough to have the privilege of paddling canoes every day. The younger children look up to the Rangers as they know when they are old enough, they too can be Rangers and have fun canoeing. There are 20 red and green canoes stored on Canoe Beach between the dock and the big rock with the YMCA symbol painted on it. They were made in Old Town, Maine, by the Old Town Canoe Company which has been making them for 75 years. Seeing the canoes being paddled on my lake is a beautiful sight.

The evenings are usually bright with stars and often the moon shines on the lake. The Rangers end their day with a bonfire beside the lake and they toast marshmallows. I am assured that one of the marshmallows will fall off a stick onto the ground and once the Rangers leave the shore, I can retrieve the fallen marshmallow and enjoy it under the stars and moon bringing an end to my perfect day.

There had been talk about two groups of children coming to Fenway Park to learn and to play baseball. Each group was coming for a week. The first group was fortunate to be helped not only by coaches from nearby schools but by legends who were retired famous baseball players. I decided the best place to view all this was beside the Monster as we were now friends and there were bleachers there where I would feel safe and not be seen. I worked my way up there Sunday night to be ready for Monday morning. There must have been 50 children of all sizes descending on the field. They were given shirts to wear and they all looked alike.

The coaches and legends were introduced to the children. There were several legends but two caught my attention. One was called Mike Torrez and he was going to help with pitching. The other was called Bucky Dent and he was going to help with shortstop play. I noticed Bucky was wearing a hat and shirt with NY on them. He was brave to come to my Fenway Park because in 1978, he was responsible for the Red Sox losing the American League East title to his New York Yankees team when he hit a home run on a pitch thrown by Red Sox pitcher Mike Torrez. The ball landed into the netting above the monster wall and the Red Sox nation has never forgotten that game. I am happy knowing that Mike and Bucky are very good friends. When the morning session was over, the children scattered for a swim and I left for the cool shade of my beautiful sanctuary and perhaps for a swim, too.

NaHa. Karate-Do. Te.

Club Naha Karate-Do Camp invaded my outdoor theater stage where they practiced karate techniques which involved kicking, jabbing and jumping to name a few. I had never seen karate before and I was curious about where and why it began.

The word karate is a Chinese word meaning "hand." Though the meaning is Chinese, karate became popular in Japan and the Japanese added "do" to karate which meant "way" as in "way of life." So, all of the Japanese martial arts are named with "do" as in Judo, Kendo and Aikido.

In 1607 the Japanese clan Satsuma invaded the island of Okinawa and took over its administration by force but the islanders had to defend themselves by hand-to-hand tactics called "Te" which means "hand" in Japanese. The art of Te differed with each location and instructors of schools teaching it. The schools were identified by the name of the city such as Naha-Te, Shuri-Te, et cetera.

It is all very complicated to me. However, when I learned that the goal of Club Naha Karate-Do is to inspire and enable the children to become productive, responsible and caring individuals, that was most important and I was very proud they were practicing and learning on my stage.

My friend Ken is called Shihan Ken which means he is a master teacher. He is well known as a master teacher because he has mastered karate. There must be a move or two he could teach me.

One day, Lester, George and Dick talked about "eating a turtle." I paid very close attention, stayed well out of sight and was relieved to hear them say how delicious the nuts, caramel and chocolate were on top of a cookie with the name of Turtle. Imagine a crustulum or cookie named after me, Turtle! It was amazing.

As fate would have it, I heard people talking about a recipe for making turtle cookies and for anyone who might like to make them, the "recipere" follows:

Turtles

Crust:
 2 c. flour
 1 c. brown sugar
 1 stick butter
 1 c. whole pecans

Caramel:
 2/3 c. butter
 ½ c. brown sugar

Topping:
 1 c. chocolate chips

350 degree oven. Parchment-lined 9"x13" pan.

Mix flour, sugar and butter at medium speed until well mixed (fine particles). Pat into pan and sprinkle pecans evenly over crust.

Caramel layer: combine brown sugar and butter. Cook over medium heat, stirring constantly, until entire surface begins to boil. Continue to boil about 1 minute, stirring constantly.

Pour caramel over crust and pecans. Bake 18-22 minutes, or until caramel is bubbly. Remove from oven and immediately sprinkle with chocolate chips. Swirl chips as they melt. Cool and cut.

When you eat your Turtle crustulum, please think of me and Lester, George and Dick and how their foray into my sanctuary was the beginning of their legacy that we have all come to love as Camp Tracy.

"Let's go, Lester and Dick." "We'll follow you, George." I watched Lester, Dick and George enter my sanctuary talking about a dream of a summer camp where children would be safe and happy playing in the summer sun. That dream became Camp Tracy which grew to include a Four Seasons Lodge, a 2/3 replica of Fenway Park, cabins to house overnight campers, an outdoor theater, tennis, and special baseball and football summer camp with coaches helping the participants.

Now it is hoped children possibly from China, Japan, Puerto Rico, Mexico and Canada will come to Fenway Park to participate in International Tournaments with our local children. To help attract friends from away and to give girls an opportunity to play softball, lacrosse and field hockey, a turf field will replace the baseball field at Fenway Park. Although there is a turf field for football, I will be especially happy with a turf baseball field because I will no longer get muddy when I cross the field to visit my Green Monster friend.

There is going to be a parking lot across from Fenway Park. The trees to be cut are to be saved for Bill Lee who used to pitch for the Boston Red Sox when he was known as "Spaceman." He was a friend of my friends, Mike Torrez and Luis Tiant. Bill is going to use the cleared parking lot trees to make baseball bats and will teach campers the magic of making a Camp Tracy tree into a Camp Tracy baseball bat. I am especially proud that trees from my sanctuary are going to be used just as they were for making the cabins.

I have been thinking that in the future there could be another baseball park across the street from the Four Seasons Lodge. Maybe a field such as Wrigley Field in Chicago and then I would not have to deal with another Monster Wall. Wrigley Field has a brick outfield wall covered with ivy and we would have an ivy-covered wall as well. Although my Fenway Monster Wall does not have a Latin name, the ivy covering the Wrigley wall does: Parthenocissus tricuspidata translates to Boston ivy and delights Monster and me because the Red Sox Fenway Park is in Boston. Since 1912, Wrigley Field is the oldest active major league ballpark after Fenway Park. They sing "Take Me Out to the Ball Game" at every game and I hope that will be done at Camp Tracy. I sing a little off-key so I must be careful.

If the new park gets built, it would be nice to dedicate it to Maine Penobscot Indian Louis Francis Sockalexis who was the grandson of a Penobscot Indian Chief and the first Native American professional baseball player. He played with the Cleveland Spiders which became the Cleveland Indians in his honor. He led the way for Native Americans Charlie Bender, John Meyers, Jim Thorpe, my friend Bucky Dent and present day Jacoby Ellsbury, former Boston Red Sox fielder of Navajo descent, to play major league baseball. A statue of Louis Francis Sockalexis representing the grace and spirit of baseball would welcome children from far and near.

In addition to baseball and other sports, I think about Camp Tracy being used all year by groups from local schools coming for such things as retreats, theater performances, concerts, and cross-country skiing. With more cabins and buildings, we could have a leadership training center as well as a recreational hall and a small gymnasium.

The dreams of Lester, Dick and George have been fulfilled beyond their imagination and now I will watch Ken and others honoring the founders of Camp Tracy as they fulfill their dreams for Camp Tracy's future.

ABOUT THE AUTHORS

I was born in Brooklyn but when I was 12, my parents moved their seven children to Amenia in upstate New York. It was there that my passion for baseball developed and remains to this day. The sand lot baseball games played there and the escapades of a group of daring teenage boys have been written up in my recently published book, *The Depot Hill Gang* (North Country Press, 2014).

I graduated from State University of New York and in January, 1985, I became the youngest director of the Boys & Girls Clubs of New Rochelle, NY, and served as Assistant Executive Director for seven years.

In 1992 I moved to Waterville and accepted the challenge to lead the Waterville area Boys & Girls Clubs as their Executive Director. Our successful fundraising was noticed by Harold Alfond who challenged me and the Board of Directors to build the best youth-serving organization and to merge with the local YMCA. I was named Chief Executive Officer of the only merged Boys & Girls Clubs and YMCA in the country.

In May of 1999 the Boys & Girls Clubs and YMCA, now known as the Alfond Youth Center, was officially opened. Youth membership has risen to over 8,000; towns served have increased to over 191 and outreach services opened other clubs throughout the state, including several on Indian Reservations.

In 2005, with the support of the New Balance Foundation, funds were raised to develop and enhance Camp Tracy. Continued fundraising enabled the Alfond Youth Center to expand by 14,000 feet.

In 2007, our team led an effort to build a replica of Fenway Park at Camp Tracy to honor Harold Alfond and his contribution to youth baseball. With the endorsement of Major League Baseball, the Red Sox Foundation, the Cal Ripken, Sr. Foundation and many others, the Harold Alfond Fenway Park was dedicated at Camp Tracy by Cal Ripken, Jr. and others on Sunday, September 9, 2007.

I've been very fortunate to have met Lester "Zayde" and Barbara "Bubbe" Jolovitz. They have of inspired me and many others and will be a part my family forever.

I live in Vassalboro, Maine, with my wife Suzanne, our son Sean and daughter Kate.

Ken Walsh, 2014

November 10, 1984. I was to be introduced to Lester T. Jolovitz on that date at an event I was to cater and he was to attend. The introduction actually never took place as we found each other. As was my wont after dessert was served, I went around offering second cups of coffee but this time I was also on a mission to try to find Lester and knew I had found him from a given description. He accepted the coffee, said the lunch was very nice (of course) and asked if I would cater for two in Waterville. Catering for two in Waterville began shortly thereafter and continued until Lester's death in February 2012.

A stranger to Waterville meant my connections were Lester's, including his association with Colby College as he was a 1939 graduate. Whereas art was an interest of mine, I became a docent at Colby's Museum of Art. The Alfond Youth Center and Camp Tracy were most important to Lester, especially Camp Tracy as one of its founders. The Jolovitz Outdoor Theater at Camp Tracy is a source of great pride to both of us. With those associations came our love for, and admiration of, Ken Walsh.

Two summers ago I wrote *Reminiscences and Recipes* (North Country Press, 2012). I was sure it was my first and last book until Ken thought we, like Turtle, should stick our necks out and collaborate on writing a history of Camp Tracy; ergo, *Behold the Turtle*. This, my second and last book, has been followed by my third and last, *A Singular Peluche*, a fantasy about a found teddy bear. *Turtle* and *Peluche* will be published by North Country Press in 2014.

Before Lester, most of my life was in Portland. I catered, taught cooking at adult education in Portland and Cape Elizabeth and did food demonstrations at The Whip and Spoon in Portland and Sterns in Waterville.

My son Karl and daughter Debbie are in the Portland area and have blessed us with grandsons Ben, Will and Nicky.

Barbara Jolovitz, 2014

ABOUT THE ILLUSTRATOR

Michael Boardman is an artist and illustrator specializing in wildlife and natural history subjects. When not drawing turtles, he runs Coyote Graphics, a screenprinting company that markets his wildlife images on shirts and cards. In addition to being an illustrator, he is a watercolor painter and has been awarded residencies at Baxter State Park and Acadia National Park.

Maine has been his home since the age of seven. He graduated from the University of Maine and is happy to be raising his own family here.

He has an affinity for reptiles and has rescued several snapping turtles from roadsides, lawns and swimming pools.

Michael Boardman, 2014